HOW TO DRAW
EXTREME
SPORTS

David Antram

BOOK HOUSE

SALARIYA

Published in Great Britain in MMXII by
Book House, an imprint of
The Salariya Book Company Ltd
25 Marlborough Place, Brighton BN1 1UB

1 3 5 7 9 8 6 4 2

Please visit our website at **www.book-house.co.uk**
or go to **www.salariya.com** for **free** electronic versions of:
You Wouldn't Want to be an Egyptian Mummy!
You Wouldn't Want to be a Roman Gladiator!
You Wouldn't Want to be a Polar Explorer!
**You Wouldn't Want to sail on a 19th-Century
   Whaling Ship!**

Author: **David Antram** was born in Brighton, England, in 1958. He studied at Eastbourne College of Art and worked in advertising for fifteen years before becoming a full-time artist. He has illustrated many children's non-fiction books.

Editor: Rob Walker

PB ISBN: 978-1-908177-17-9

A CIP catalogue record for this book is available from the British Library.

Printed and bound in China.
Printed on paper from sustainable sources.

WARNING: Fixatives should be used only under adult supervision.

Visit our websites to read interactive free web books, stay up to date with new releases, catch up with us on the Book House Blog, view our electronic catalogue and more!

www.book-house.co.uk
Information books
and graphic novels

www.scribblersbooks.com
Books for babies, toddlers and
pre-school children.

Follow us on Facebook and
Twitter by visiting
www.salariya.com

PAPER FROM
SUSTAINABLE
FORESTS

Contents

Making a start

Learning to draw is about looking and seeing. Keep practising and get to know your subject.

Use a sketchbook to make quick sketches. Start by doodling and experimenting with shapes and patterns. There are many ways to draw; this book shows one method. Visit art galleries, look at artists' drawings, see how friends draw, but above all, find your own way.

Use simple shapes to draw the figure in action with their equipment.

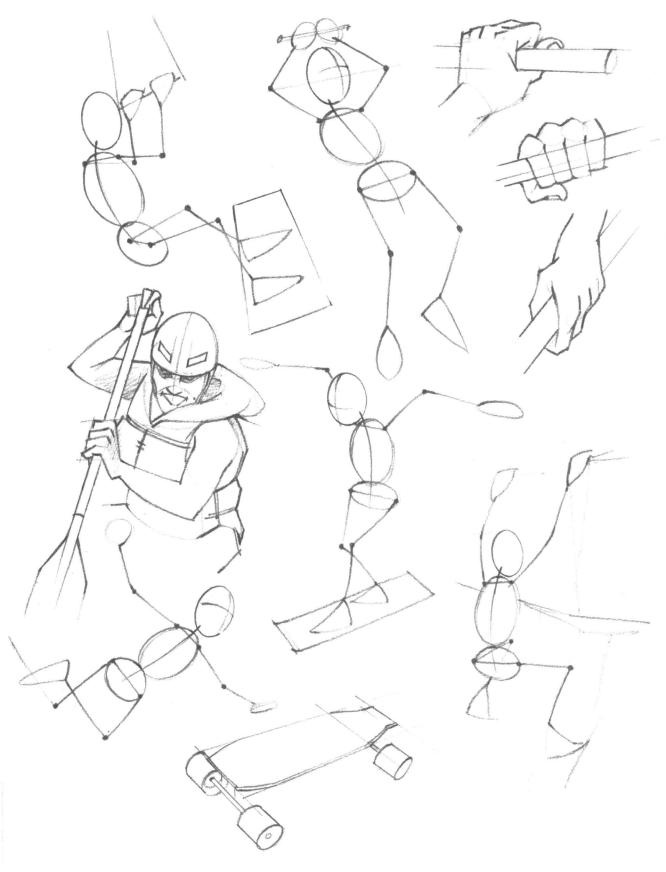

Perspective

If you look at any object from different viewpoints, you will see that the part that is closest to you looks larger, and the part furthest away from you looks smaller. Drawing in perspective is a way of creating a feeling of space — of showing three dimensions on a flat surface.

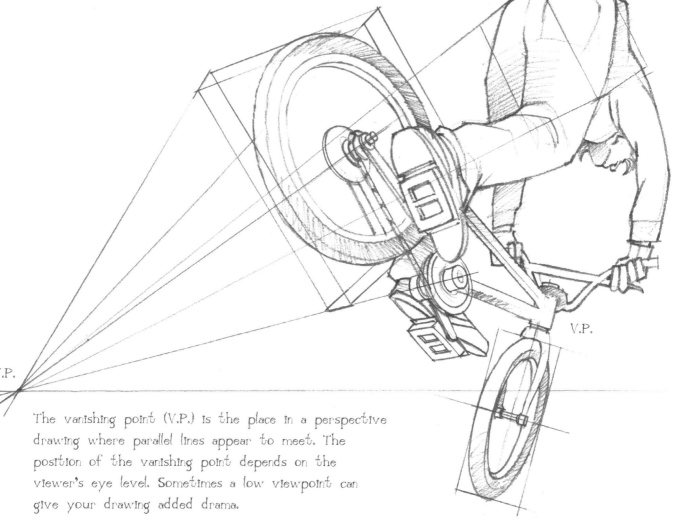

The vanishing point (V.P.) is the place in a perspective drawing where parallel lines appear to meet. The position of the vanishing point depends on the viewer's eye level. Sometimes a low viewpoint can give your drawing added drama.

V.P.

V.P.

6

Two-point perspective drawing

Low eye level
(view from below)

Two-point perspective uses two vanishing points: one for lines running along the length of the subject, and one on the opposite side for lines running across the width of the object.

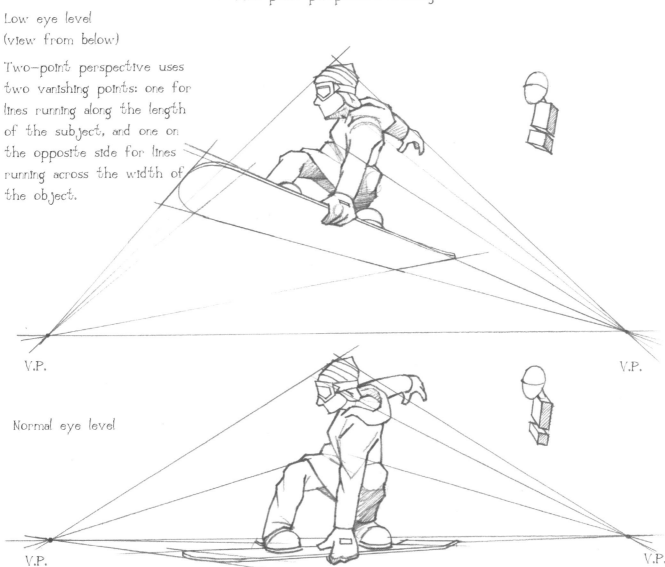

V.P.   V.P.

Normal eye level

V.P.   V.P.

High eye level
(view from above)

V.P.   V.P.

V.P. = vanishing point

7

Drawing tools

Here are just a few of the many tools that you can use for drawing. Let your imagination go, and have fun experimenting with all the different marks you can make.

Pencil

Watercolour pencil

Charcoal pencil

Charcoal stick

Pastels

Finger painting

Black, grey and white pastel on grey sugar paper

Each grade of **pencil** makes a different mark, from fine, grey lines through to soft, black ones. Hard pencils are graded as H, 2H, 3H, 4H, 5H and 6H (the hardest). An HB pencil is ideal for general sketching. Soft pencils are graded from B, 2B, 3B, 4B, 5B to 6B (the softest and blackest).

Watercolour pencils come in many different colours and make a line similar to an HB pencil. But paint over your finished drawing with clean water, and the lines will soften and run.

It is less messy and easier to achieve a fine line with a **charcoal pencil** than a stick of charcoal. Create soft tones by smudging lines with your finger. **Ask an adult** to spray the drawing with fixative to prevent further smudging.

Pastels are brittle sticks of powdered colour. They blend and smudge easily and are ideal for quick sketches. Pastel drawings work well on textured, coloured paper. **Ask an adult** to spray your finished drawing with fixative.

Experiment with **finger painting**. Your fingerprints make exciting patterns and textures. Use your fingers to smudge soft pencil, charcoal and pastel lines.

8

Ballpoint pens are very useful for sketching and making notes. Make different tones by building up layers of shading.

A **mapping pen** has to be dipped into bottled ink to fill the nib. Different nib shapes make different marks. Try putting a diluted ink wash over parts of the finished drawing.

Draughtsmen's pens and specialist **art pens** can produce extremely fine lines and are ideal for creating surface texture. A variety of pen nibs are available which produce different widths of line.

Felt-tip pens are ideal for quick sketches. If the ink is not waterproof, try drawing on wet paper and see what happens.

Broad-nibbed **marker pens** make interesting lines and are good for large, bold sketches. Try using a black pen for the main sketch and a grey one to block in areas of shadow.

Paintbrushes are shaped differently to make different marks. Japanese brushes are soft and produce beautiful flowing lines. Large sable brushes are good for painting a wash over a line drawing. Fine brushes are good for drawing delicate lines.

9

Materials

Try using different types of drawing papers and materials. Experiment with charcoal, wax crayons and pastels. All pens, from felt-tips to ballpoints, will make interesting marks. Try drawing with pen and ink on wet paper.

Ink silhouette

Silhouette is a style of drawing which mainly uses solid black shapes.

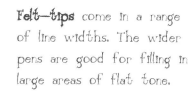

Felt-tips come in a range of line widths. The wider pens are good for filling in large areas of flat tone.

Remember, the best equipment and materials will not necessarily make the best drawing – only practice will!

Pencil drawings can include a vast amount of detail and tone. Try experimenting with the different grades of pencil to get a range of light and shade effects in your drawing.

Hatching

Lines drawn in **ink** cannot be erased, so keep your ink drawings sketchy and less rigid. Don't worry about mistakes, as these can be lost in the drawing as it develops.

It can be tricky adding light and shade to a drawing with a pen. Use a solid layer of ink for the very darkest areas and cross–hatching (straight lines criss–crossing each other) for ordinary dark tones. Hatching (straight lines running parallel to each other) can be used for midtones.

Cross–hatching

11

Wheels

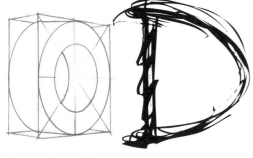

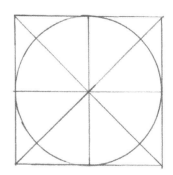

Fit the circle in the box.

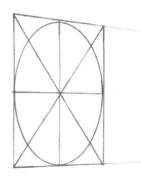

As the square turns into a perspective viewpoint, the circle becomes an ellipse.

Drawing wheels from different perspectives can be tricky. The solution is to use construction lines to draw a square or perspective box, then fit the wheel within it.

First draw a perspective box with vertical and horizontal lines running through the centre. Draw in the perimeter of the wheel, paying attention to the construction lines to make sure it touches at the edges of the perspective box, top, bottom, left and right. Add an inner ellipse for the inside of the wheel.

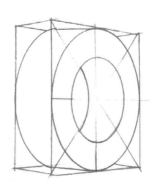

Examples of different perspective wheels and the construction boxes needed:

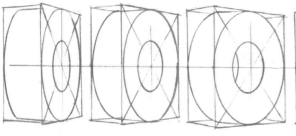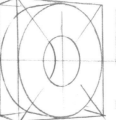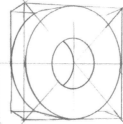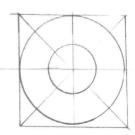

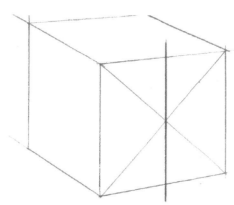

How to find the centre point.

To find the centre point of the perspective box, simply draw two lines from corner to corner. The point where they cross is the centre. Use this point to add your centre lines.

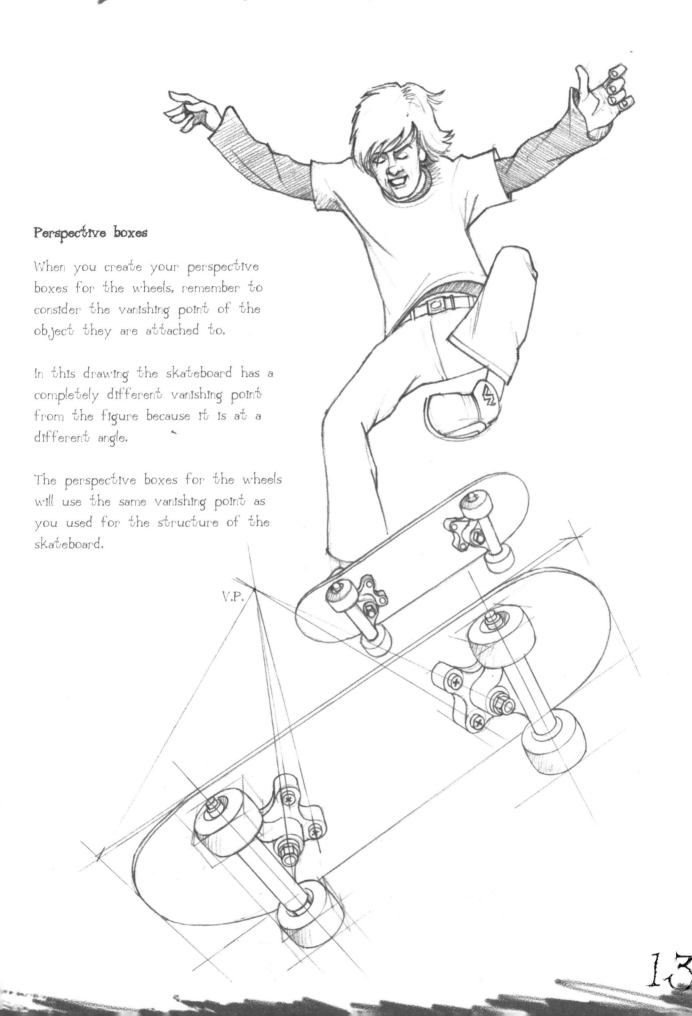

Perspective boxes

When you create your perspective boxes for the wheels, remember to consider the vanishing point of the object they are attached to.

In this drawing the skateboard has a completely different vanishing point from the figure because it is at a different angle.

The perspective boxes for the wheels will use the same vanishing point as you used for the structure of the skateboard.

V.P.

Dramatic heights

The choice of background can often add tension and drama to extreme sports. Here are two sports seen from a great height. The use of perspective drawing in relation to the figure gives a great sense of height and danger.

The climber clings perilously to a rock face. Use perspective to show how steep the rock face is as it falls away into the distance.

Add shading to areas where the light wouldn't reach to help create a three-dimensional effect.

The parachutist falls to a faraway airfield.

Use perspective to draw in the airfield in relation to the falling parachutist.

Consider the scale of the buildings to show how far below the airfield is.

When your drawing is complete, remove unwanted construction lines.

15

Freestyle BMX

The BMX is the perfect bike for freestyling. With pegs attached and a flexible setup, riders are capable of performing amazing tricks and stunts.

Start by drawing the rider as a simple stick figure with dots to indicate joints.

Add ovals for the head, body, hips and hands.

Draw simple triangles for the feet.

Using straight lines mark out the frame of the BMX.

Using the construction lines as a guide, add tube shapes for the legs and circles for knees.

Sketch in the position of the facial features.

Using the construction lines as a guide, add tube shapes for the arms with circles for elbows.

Add more detail to the shape of the feet.

Add the BMX wheels to the bike frame.

Add parts of the frame and pegs.

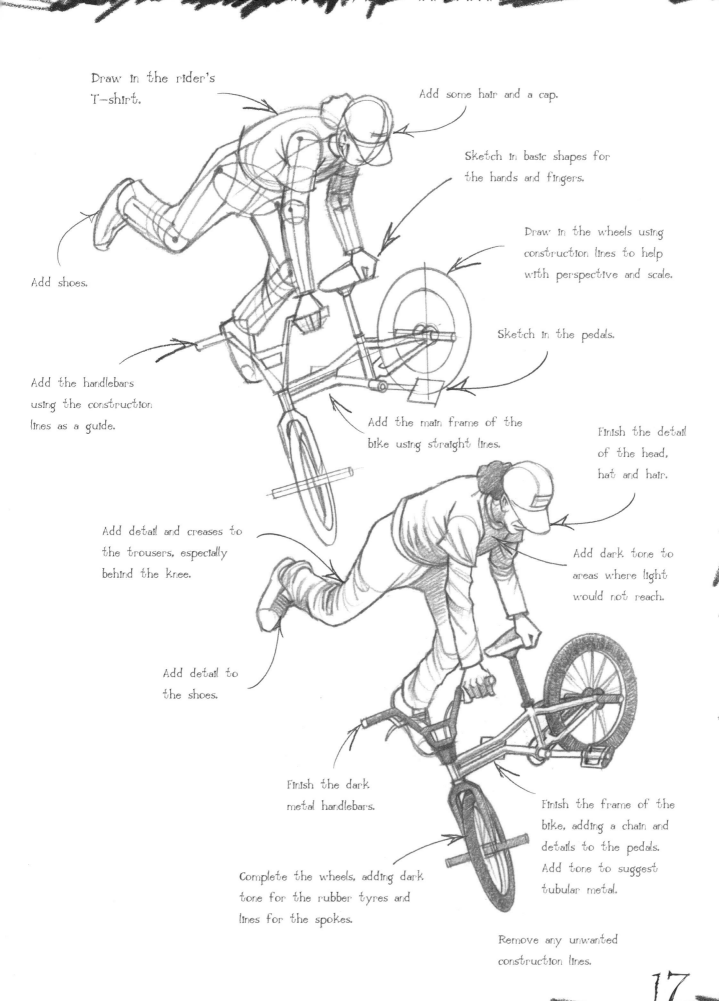

Draw in the rider's
T-shirt.

Add some hair and a cap.

Sketch in basic shapes for
the hands and fingers.

Draw in the wheels using
construction lines to help
with perspective and scale.

Add shoes.

Sketch in the pedals.

Add the handlebars
using the construction
lines as a guide.

Add the main frame of the
bike using straight lines.

Finish the detail
of the head,
hat and hair.

Add detail and creases to
the trousers, especially
behind the knee.

Add dark tone to
areas where light
would not reach.

Add detail to
the shoes.

Finish the dark
metal handlebars.

Finish the frame of the
bike, adding a chain and
details to the pedals.
Add tone to suggest
tubular metal.

Complete the wheels, adding dark
tone for the rubber tyres and
lines for the spokes.

Remove any unwanted
construction lines.

17

Skysurfing

Skysurfing is a high-altitude extreme sport. A skysurfer freefalls from an aeroplane with a board attached to his feet, surfing the air and performing stunts on the way to the ground.

Start by sketching in a simple stick figure with dots for the joints.

Draw ovals for the head, body, hips and hands.

Draw in the shape of the hands.

Draw in simple tube shapes for the arms. Add circles for the elbows.

Position basic facial features and add a neck.

Connect the body and hip ovals together.

Sketch in tube shapes for the legs and attach them to the hip oval.

This arm and hand are shortened because of perspective.

Add circles for the knees.

Sketch in the board.

18

Add fingers to the hand.

Draw in the rounded helmet.

Using the construction lines as a guide, sketch in the skydiving suit around the body.

Sketch in more detail to the facial features and add goggles.

Add the parachute and its straps.

Add crease lines in the skydiving suit.

Complete the details of the helmet and face.

Draw in the feet.

Add the shape of the board.

Add tone to the parachute and its straps.

Use shading to indicate creases and folds in fabric.

Add tone for the pattern of the suit.

Extreme angles

Drawing your extreme sport taking place at extreme angles can give your drawing added drama.

Complete the feet strapped to the board.

Remove any unwanted construction lines.

19

ATV racing

These powerful quad bikes are adapted to be fast, lightweight and manoeuvrable for many different types of racing. ATV stands for All Terrain Vehicle.

Sketch in a simple seated stick figure with dots for the joints.

Draw two straight lines to position the front and rear wheels.

Sketch in the main chassis of the ATV.

Add the shape of the wheels (see page 12).

Sketch in some facial features.

Using the construction lines as a guide, draw in tube-shaped arms and legs, adding circles at the knees and elbows.

Add detail to the main chassis of the ATV.

Define the shape of the wheels.

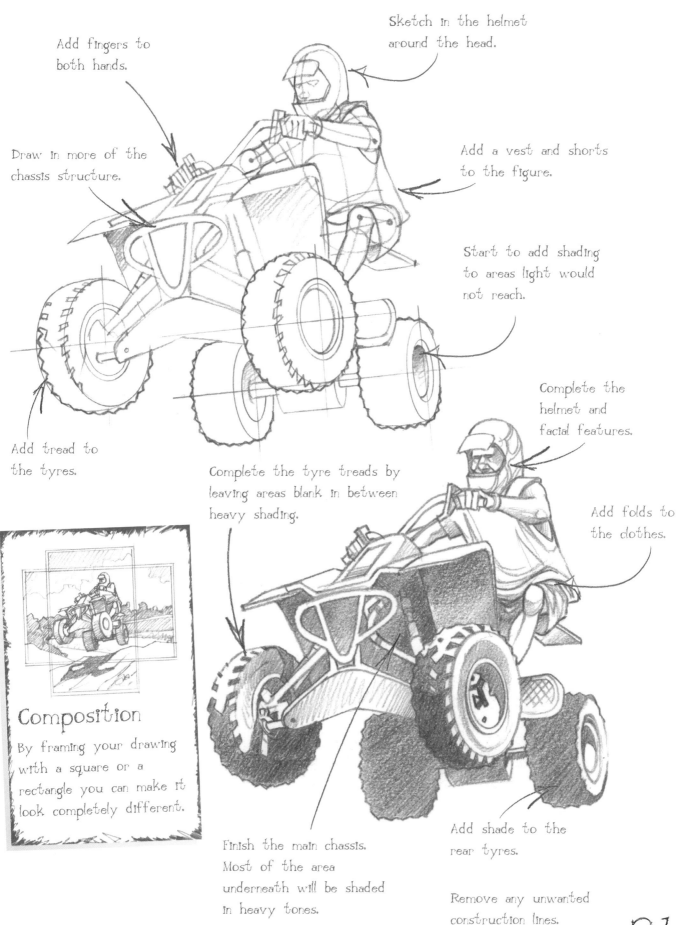

Sketch in the helmet around the head.

Add fingers to both hands.

Draw in more of the chassis structure.

Add a vest and shorts to the figure.

Start to add shading to areas light would not reach.

Add tread to the tyres.

Complete the tyre treads by leaving areas blank in between heavy shading.

Complete the helmet and facial features.

Add folds to the clothes.

Composition

By framing your drawing with a square or a rectangle you can make it look completely different.

Finish the main chassis. Most of the area underneath will be shaded in heavy tones.

Add shade to the rear tyres.

Remove any unwanted construction lines.

21

Wakeboarding

This extreme watersport involves being towed behind a boat at high speeds on a small wakeboard. Hitting the wake of the boat enables the wakeboarder to fly into the air and perform amazing tricks.

Draw ovals for the head, body and hands.

Add a line for the tow rope handle.

Start by sketching in a simple stick figure with dots for the joints.

Add the shape of the feet.

Sketch in simple tube shapes for the arms.

Add some facial details.

Add circles for elbows.

Draw two parallel lines for the wakeboard.

Draw in the hand shapes.

Draw in simple tube shapes for the legs, adding circles for knees.

Add more shape to the feet.

Add curved, windswept lines for hair.

Using the construction lines as a guide, add the curved shape of the arms.

Sketch in the tow rope.

Add fingers to the hands.

Draw a vest on the figure.

Draw a basic boot shape around the feet.

Add long, baggy shorts.

Add tone to define muscle structure.

Finish the details of the tow rope and handle.

Complete the details of the head and hair.

Complete the shorts with a graphic design and creases.

Finish the boot details.

Add folds and creases to the vest.

Add the waves and splash of water.

Complete the wakeboard.

Remove any unwanted construction lines.

23

Skateboarding

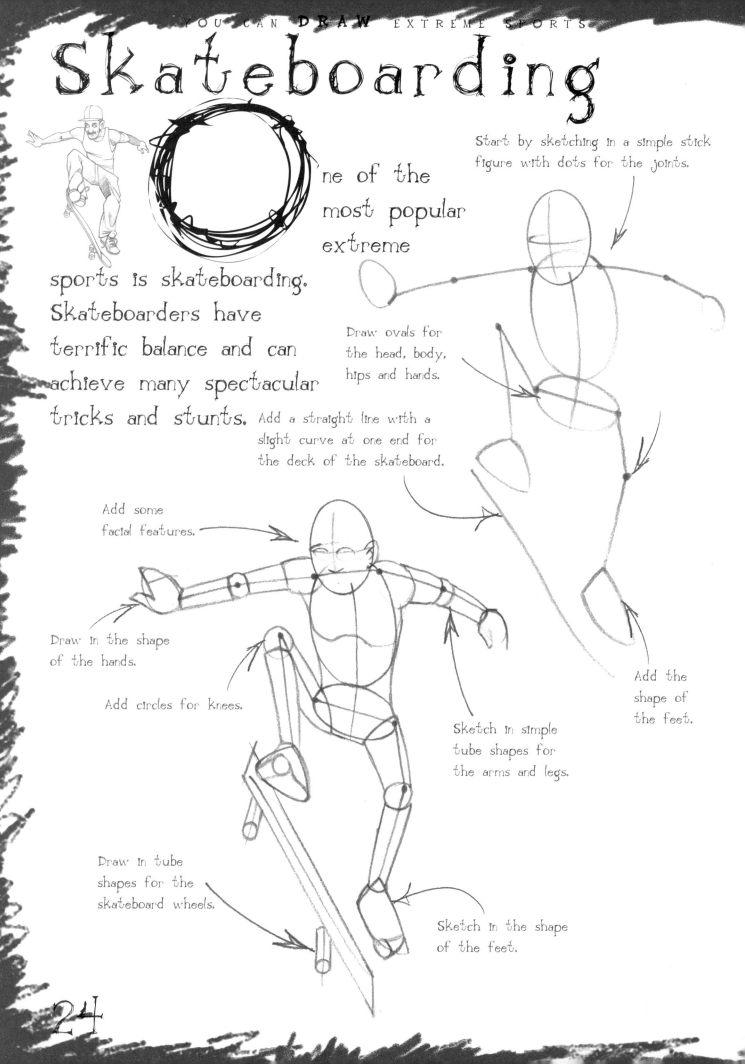

One of the most popular extreme sports is skateboarding. Skateboarders have terrific balance and can achieve many spectacular tricks and stunts.

Start by sketching in a simple stick figure with dots for the joints.

Draw ovals for the head, body, hips and hands.

Add a straight line with a slight curve at one end for the deck of the skateboard.

Add some facial features.

Draw in the shape of the hands.

Add circles for knees.

Sketch in simple tube shapes for the arms and legs.

Add the shape of the feet.

Draw in tube shapes for the skateboard wheels.

Sketch in the shape of the feet.

Draw in
the fingers.

Add a cap to
the head.

Draw in both arms using the
construction lines as a guide. This
arm is very foreshortened because
of its angle.

Sketch in
the trousers.

Add a vest.

Separate the
tube into
individual wheels.

Add muscle detail
to the arms.

Complete the
facial details.

Start to draw in the
skateboarder's shoes.

Add dark
tone to
areas where
light would
not reach.

Add creases to
the trouser fabric.

Finish drawing
the skateboard.

Shadows
Adding a shadow to your
drawing can give it added
drama. The shape of the
skater's shadow will
depend on the direction
of the light source.

Finish drawing the
skateboard shoes,
adding laces and detail.

Remove any unwanted
construction lines.

25

Skydiving

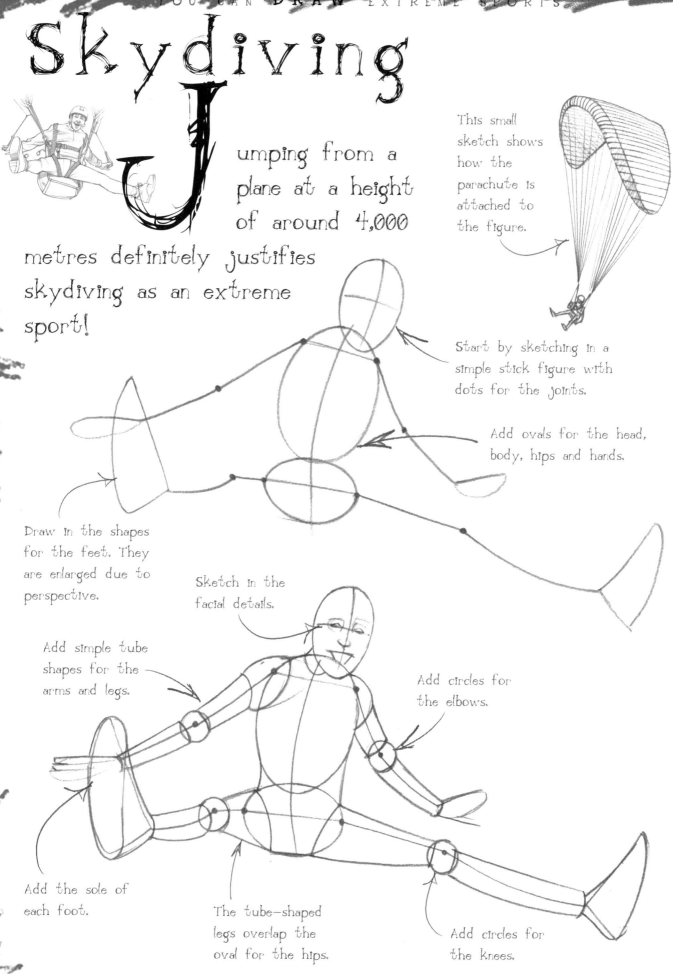

Jumping from a plane at a height of around 4,000 metres definitely justifies skydiving as an extreme sport!

This small sketch shows how the parachute is attached to the figure.

Start by sketching in a simple stick figure with dots for the joints.

Add ovals for the head, body, hips and hands.

Draw in the shapes for the feet. They are enlarged due to perspective.

Sketch in the facial details.

Add simple tube shapes for the arms and legs.

Add circles for the elbows.

Add the sole of each foot.

The tube-shaped legs overlap the oval for the hips.

Add circles for the knees.

26

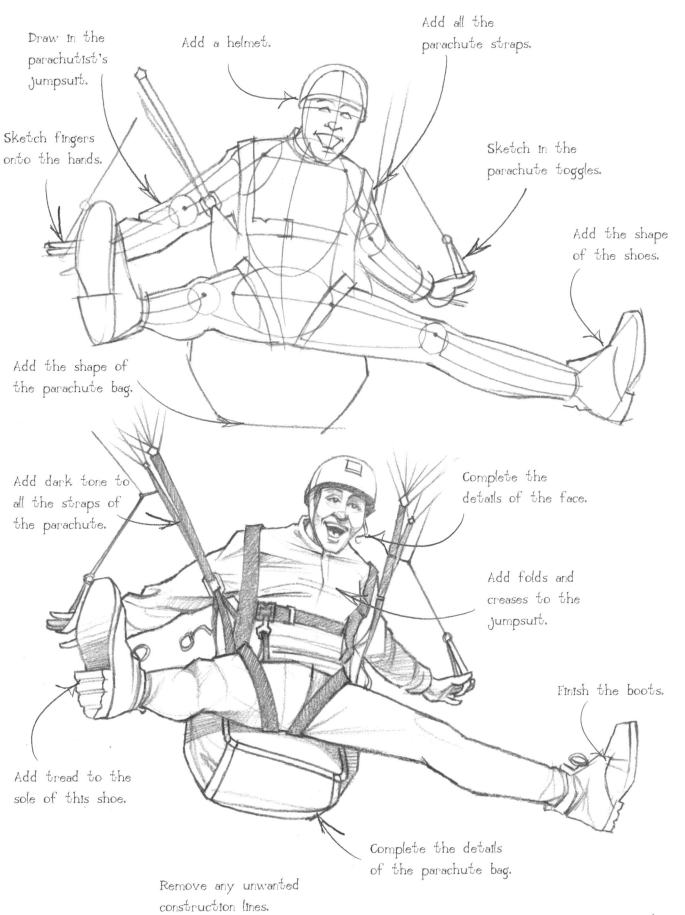

Draw in the parachutist's jumpsuit.

Add a helmet.

Add all the parachute straps.

Sketch fingers onto the hands.

Sketch in the parachute toggles.

Add the shape of the shoes.

Add the shape of the parachute bag.

Add dark tone to all the straps of the parachute.

Complete the details of the face.

Add folds and creases to the jumpsuit.

Finish the boots.

Add tread to the sole of this shoe.

Complete the details of the parachute bag.

Remove any unwanted construction lines.

27

River rafting

River rafting is an extreme water sport. Each team will try to successfully navigate a rubber raft down fast flowing rivers and through rapids.

Sketch in five seated stick figures with dots for the joints.

Draw ovals for the heads, bodies and hands of all five figures.

Draw in a line between each figure's hands for the paddle handles.

Sketch in some curved lines to position the raft.

Add simple, tube-shaped arms for each figure.

Add circles for elbows and knees.

Add the blades of the paddles.

Sketch in more of the upper raft using curved lines.

Draw in simple tube-shaped legs.

28

Add helmets to
each of the heads.

Sketch in the bulky life
jackets around each figure.

Add more detail
to the paddles.

Add facial details.

Draw in the shape
of the fingers.

Add more detail
to the boat.

Complete the
facial features.

Add final details to the
helmets and life jackets.

Add dark
tone to areas
where light
would not reach.

Add lots of curving
lines to create rushing
water and splashes.

Add tone to show
muscle structure.

Finish the raft by adding
tone in different areas.

Remove any unwanted
construction lines.

29

Kitesurfing

Kitesurfing uses the power of the wind. It propels the kitesurfer across the surface of the water at high speeds before he leaps, wind—aided, many metres into the air.

Start with a simple stick figure with dots for joints.

Draw in a line for the kite handle.

Bend one leg behind the other.

Mark the position of the board.

Add ovals for the feet.

Draw ovals for the body, head and hips.

Add detail to the shape of the hands.

Add simple, tube—shaped arms.

Draw circles for the elbows and knees.

Join the two main ovals for the body.

Attach the feet to the board.

Sketch in some facial features.

Add simple, tube—shaped legs coming from the hips.

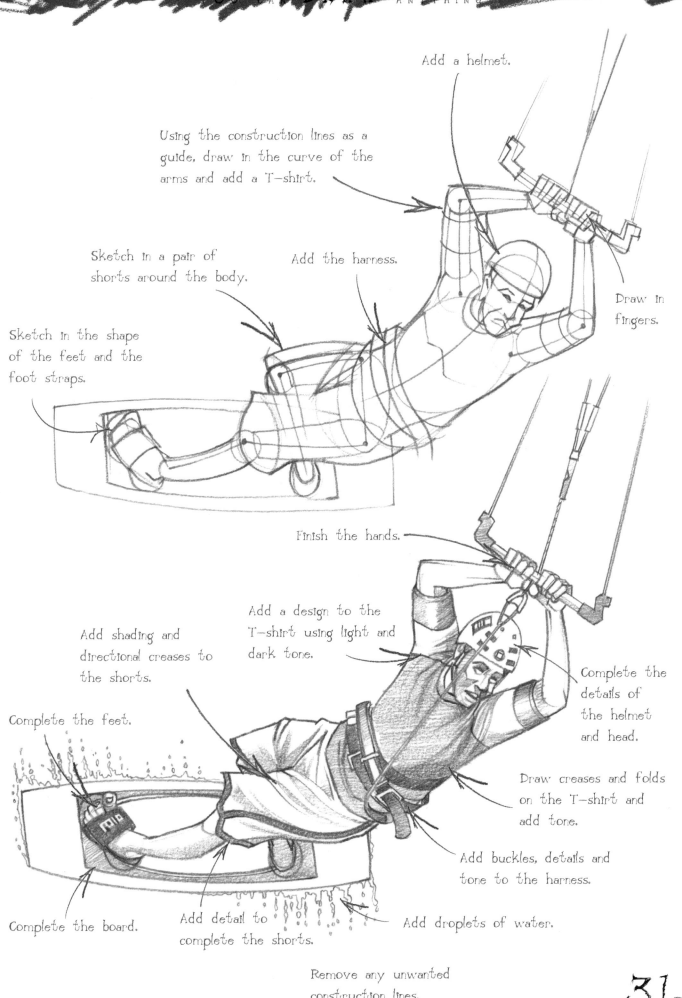

Add a helmet.

Using the construction lines as a guide, draw in the curve of the arms and add a T-shirt.

Sketch in a pair of shorts around the body.

Add the harness.

Draw in fingers.

Sketch in the shape of the feet and the foot straps.

Finish the hands.

Add a design to the T-shirt using light and dark tone.

Add shading and directional creases to the shorts.

Complete the details of the helmet and head.

Complete the feet.

Draw creases and folds on the T-shirt and add tone.

Add buckles, details and tone to the harness.

Complete the board.

Add detail to complete the shorts.

Add droplets of water.

Remove any unwanted construction lines.

Glossary

Composition The positioning of a picture on the drawing paper.

Construction lines Guidelines used in the early stages of a drawing which are usually erased later.

Cross–hatching A series of criss–crossing lines used to add shade to a drawing.

Fixative A type of resin used to spray over a finished drawing to prevent smudging. **It should only be used by an adult.**

Hatching A series of parallel lines used to add shade to a drawing.

Light source The direction from which the light seems to come in a drawing.

Reference Photographs or other images used to help produce a drawing, if drawing from life is not possible.

Silhouette A drawing that shows only a dark shape, like a shadow.

Three–dimensional Having an effect of depth, so as to look lifelike or real.

Vanishing point The place in a perspective drawing where parallel lines appear to meet.

Index